The Ultimate Self-Teaching Method! Level One

Play Violin Today!

A Complete Guide to the Basics

To access audio visit:
www.halleonard.com/mylibrary

Enter Code
7335-0088-6768-2562

by Sharon Stosur

Recorded at BeatHouse, Milwaukee, Wisconsin

Jerry Loughney, violin
Warren Wiegratz, keyboards
Jim Reith, guitars

ISBN 978-1-4234-0442-2

HAL•LEONARD® CORPORATION

7777 W. BLUEMOUND RD. P.O. BOX 13819 MILWAUKEE, WI 53213

Visit Hal Leonard Online at
www.halleonard.com

Introduction

Welcome to *Play Violin Today!*—the series designed to prepare you for any style of violin playing, from classical to folk to country. Whatever your taste in music, *Play Violin Today!* will give you the start you need.

About the Audio

It's easy and fun to play the violin, and the accompanying online audio will make your learning even more enjoyable, as we take you step by step through each lesson and play each song along with full accompaniment. Much like a real lesson, the best way to learn this material is to first read and practice on your own, then listen to the audio. With *Play Violin Today!*, you can learn at your own pace. If there is ever something you don't quite understand the first time through, go back to the audio and listen again. Every musical track has been given a number, so if you want to practice a song again, you can find it right away.

Contents

The Basics

The Parts of the Violin

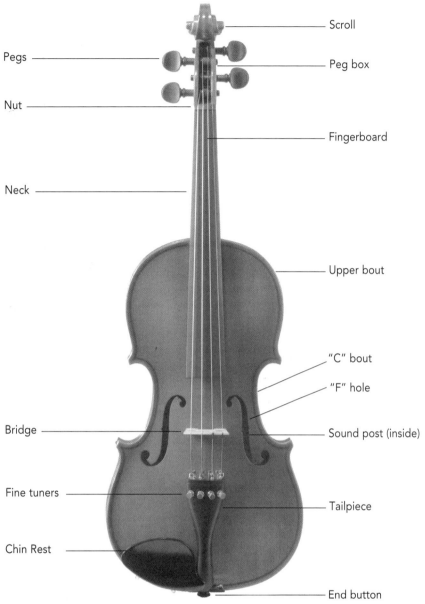

Scroll

Pegs

Peg box

Nut

Fingerboard

Neck

Upper bout

"C" bout

"F" hole

Bridge

Sound post (inside)

Fine tuners

Tailpiece

Chin Rest

End button

The Bow

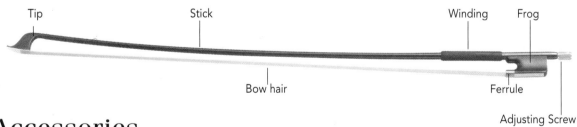

Tip Stick Winding Frog

Bow hair Ferrule

Adjusting Screw

Accessories

You will also need rosin for your bow, and a soft cloth for removing fingerprints and rosin dust before putting your violin back in the case. You may wish to use a shoulder rest to help hold the violin more comfortably. Shoulder rests attach to the underside of your violin and can be purchased at your local music store, available in a variety of materials and styles. Some string players use a soft sponge or cloth in place of the shoulder rest. A shoulder rest is not required to hold the violin properly, but many players find them to be helpful. You may wish to experiment with several types to decide what works best for you.

Holding Your Violin

With the left hand, pick up your violin by the neck with the strings facing away from you. Hold the instrument where the neck meets the body. If you grab it too close to the pegs, you may "bump" them, throwing the instrument out of tune.

Turn the violin toward you, with the strings facing the ceiling. Bring the violin to your left shoulder placing the side of your left jaw against the chin rest, creating a slight angle between your face and the violin, with the violin angling to the left.

Although it is called a chin rest, your chin never rests directly on the chin rest, rather your jaw is what comes most in contact with it. Slide your right hand toward the pegs, stopping about 1½ inches in front of the nut. Curve your fingers slightly around the neck to touch the strings. Your thumb remains unbent, resting against the left side of the neck. Your left hand cradles the neck in this way, however it does not support the weight of your instrument. Your shoulder and chin support and hold the instrument. Your left wrist should be straight, and your left arm and elbow should be directly beneath the middle of the violin. Practice holding the violin under your chin without your left hand for several seconds, gradually adding to the amount of time you can support the violin

without your left hand. Try to keep your neck and shoulder as relaxed as possible while still supporting the weight of the violin. You may find that a soft sponge or shoulder rest attached beneath the violin will help cushion the space between the violin and your shoulder. This can help make holding the violin more comfortable.

The Bow

Preparing Your Bow

When a bow is stored in its case, the hair is loosened. After taking the bow from your case to play, you will need to tighten the hair by turning the screw clockwise, until the hair is straight and firm, still leaving the stick visibly bowed. Take care not to over tighten the hair, which could damage the bow and produce a harsh sound.

Before playing, rosin the bow by holding the rosin in your left hand while sliding the bow back and forth across the rosin, moving the bow and holding the rosin steady. You will need to apply a little rosin each time you take your violin out to play.

Remember to loosen the bow hair by turning the screw counterclockwise before putting the bow back in the case again.

Holding the Bow

As you learn to hold the bow for the first time, put down your violin so your left hand can assist you. As you become more comfortable with your bow, you will be able to pick it up easily with your right hand alone.

Using your left hand, pick up the bow in the middle of the stick with the hair facing the floor. You should always avoid touching the hair. Place the tip of your right thumb against the spot where the left end of the frog meets the stick, bending your thumb joint slightly.

Allow your middle and ring fingers to curve over the stick—your middle finger roughly opposite your thumb, touching the ferrule. The first joint of your index finger will rest along the top of the stick in the middle of the winding, and the tip of your little finger will rest on top of the stick near the screw. Your hand should be relaxed with the fingers spread comfortably. You will want to practice finding this position several times each day until it becomes easy.

The hair should still be facing the floor. Carefully let go of the stick with your left hand. You will notice the weighty feeling on the frog side of the bow.

Learning to properly hold the bow takes a little patience and practice. As you begin to learn notes on the violin, you may wish to pluck the string first, instead of using the bow right away. Plucking a stringed instrument is called "pizzicato." As you play new notes and pieces pizzicato, continue to practice holding the bow to become more comfortable with it.

Tuning Your Violin

The four strings on the violin are tuned to the following pitches, from bottom (low) to top (high): G, D, A, E.

You can adjust each pitch by tightening or loosening each string by turning its corresponding peg. You can make very small adjustments to the string by turning the fine tuners. To tune your violin it is easiest to use an electronic tuner or a piano or keyboard. You may also use a pitch pipe or tuning fork. The online audio will also enable you to tune your violin. Listen to each pitch, starting with the highest, and adjust the strings as necessary to match the pitches. Always tune your instrument before playing.

Violin Care Tip

When placing the violin back in its case, always wipe the rosin off the strings with a soft cloth. This will ensure a longer string life. Also, to protect the wood of the instrument, it is good to place a humidifier in the case during the colder months of the year. Ask for a violin humidifier at your local music store.

 # Tuning the E string:

Rest your violin on your knees with the strings facing you. Listen to the E on audio, electric tuner, or piano. Pluck the E on your violin to determine if it matches the E being played. Raise the pitch by turning the corresponding peg slowly and carefully *away* from you. Lower the pitch by turning the peg slowly and carefully **toward** you. If the pitch is very close, use the fine tuner to a make a smaller adjustment. (Not all violins come equipped with fine tuners on all four strings. As a beginner, it is recommended you have a fine tuner on each string.) Turning the fine tuner clockwise **raises** the pitch, counterclockwise **lowers** the pitch. Continue tuning the other three strings in the same manner.

Some Tuning Tips:

While tightening or loosening a string, turn the peg or fine tuner slowly, concentrating on the changes in pitch. You might need to pluck the string repeatedly to compare the sound of your string to the note you are tuning to.

As you're tuning a string, you may notice a series of pulsating beat waves. These beat waves can help you tune; they'll slow down as the pitches get closer together, stopping completely when the two pitches are the same, meaning they are in tune.

Instead of tuning a string down to a pitch, tune it up. This allows you to stretch the string into place, which will help it stay in tune longer. If a string is too high in pitch, tune it down first, then bring it back up to pitch. Always be careful not to tune a string too high or too quickly. Strings can break easily as a result, especially the E string.

Reading Music

Musical sounds are indicated by symbols called **notes**. The two most important components to every note are **pitch** and **rhythm**.

Pitch

Pitch (the highness or lowness of a note) is indicated by the horizontal placement of a note on the staff. Notes higher on the staff are higher in pitch. To name the pitches, we use the first seven letters of the alphabet: A, B, C, D, E, F, and G. The treble clef ⋆** assigns a particular pitch name to each line and space on the staff, centered around the pitch G, located on the second line from the bottom. Music for violin is always written in the treble clef. (Depending on range, some instruments use other clefs. The cello, for example, a lower sounding instrument, uses the bass clef.)

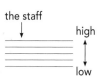

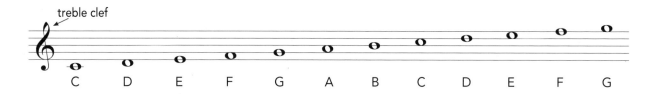

An easy way to remember the pitches on the lines is "**E**very **G**ood **B**oy **D**oes **F**ine." For the spaces, spell "FACE."

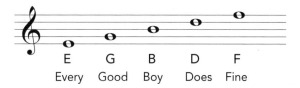

Rhythm

Rhythm refers to the elements of time—how long, or for how many beats a note lasts, including spaces or rests in between notes. Notes of different durations are represented by the following symbols:

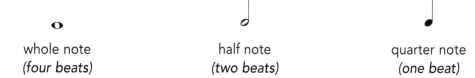

whole note *(four beats)*   half note *(two beats)*   quarter note *(one beat)*

To help you keep track of beats in a piece of music, the staff is divided into measures (or "bars"). A time signature (or "meter") at the beginning of the staff indicates how many beats you can expect to find in each measure.

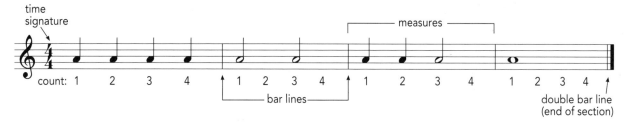

4/4 is perhaps the most common time signature. The top number indicates how many beats there are in each measure. The bottom number shows what kind of note value receives one beat ("4" is most often on the bottom, but numbers such as "8" or even "2" are used as well). In 4/4 time, there are four beats in each measure, and each beat is worth one quarter note.

four beats per measure
quarter note (♩) = one beat

three beats per measure
quarter note (♩) = one beat

Accidentals

Any note can be raised or lowered a half step by placing an **accidental** directly before it.

Sharp (♯)   ⟶   Raises a note one half step

Flat (♭)   ⟶   Lowers a note one half step

Natural (♮)   ⟶   Cancels previously used sharp or flat

Open Strings

From lowest to highest, the strings on the violin are: G D A E.

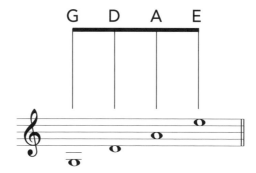

Memorize the names of the strings and their corresponding notes on the staff by playing the notes *pizzicato* (plucked, often abbreviated as *pizz.*). With your violin in proper position on your left shoulder, place your right thumb against the lower right hand corner of the fingerboard under the E string. Use your index finger to pluck each of the open strings. A gentle but firm plucking motion will produce a good tone.

Pizzicato vs. Arco

Usually, when no instruction is given as to whether or not the tune should be plucked or bowed, it is assumed that bowing will be used. The term **arco** (with the bow) is usually used to instruct the player to start using the bow after a passage that was just played ***pizzicato***.

Note Names

Say the names of the open strings aloud as you play "Open String Pizzicato" and "Open String Challenge." Doing so will help you learn the letter names on the staff faster. Feel free to sing them as well.

Open String Pizzicato

▶ If you pluck too hard, the string will snap back against the fingerboard producing a loud, percussive sound (snap pizz.).

0 = open string

Open String Challenge

Placing the Bow on the Strings

Hold your violin in its proper position with your left hand, and your bow in your right hand. Place the hair of the bow, starting near the frog, on the D string, about halfway between the bridge and the end of the fingerboard (slightly closer to the brige). Your bow arm should be bent at about a 90 degree angle. Draw the bow across the string, opening your arm from the elbow in a downward motion toward the floor. This is called "down bow." Use enough weight on the string to create a ringing tone.

Now close your arm from the elbow bringing the bow back across the string, moving the bow toward you in an upward, or opposite motion. This is called "up bow." Practice bowing each open string to become comfortable with the down bow and up bow motions. If you become tense or tired while practicing, stop and rest a few moments before you resume.

⊓ = **down bow**: drawing the bow downward, towards the floor

V = **up bow**: drawing the bow upward, towards you

Bowing on Open Strings

As you play "Open String Bowing," use a down bow for the first half note in each measure, and an up bow for the second half note in each measure. When you see the indication *arco* in the music, it means to play with the bow on the string.

 # Open String Bowing

Raise and lower your arm slightly as you move from string to string. Keep your bow halfway between the bridge and the end of the fingerboard. If you find your bow creeping down toward the bridge, slow down.

More Open Strings

Practice check list:

- Proper violin position
- Relaxed bow hold
- Bow placed halfway between bridge and fingerboard
- Slight arm shift from string to string
- Steady quarter-note beat

"Open String Warm Up" can be used as a daily warm up. Play it *pizzicato* first, and then use your bow.

 # Open String Warm Up

Lesson 3 Notes on the D String

New Note: E

The note E sounds a whole step above the open D string. Place your first finger on the D string about 1 ¼ inches below the nut to sound the note E. Your nail should be facing you. Keep your other fingers curved over the strings but not touching the strings, being careful not to let the little finger curl under the fingerboard.

E

Whole Steps and Half Steps

Whole step: two half steps, or the distance between two white keys (with a black key in between) on a piano keyboard. The first three notes of a major scale (do-re-mi) are whole steps.

Half Step: the smallest distance in traditional music, or the distance from one white key to the closest possible key (black or white), with no keys in between, on the keyboard.

First Finger on D String

As you play "Aiming for E" (pizzicato), concentrate on the sound of the whole step between open D string and first finger E. Determine exactly where your first finger should be placed to sound a whole step higher.

Aiming for E

New Note: F#

A sharp symbol (#) raises a note a half step. Placing a sharp on the staff before F raises the note, making it F sharp. F# sounds a whole step higher than first finger E. To play F#, place your second finger about one inch from the first finger, keeping your first finger on E.

Memorize where the first and second fingers are placed to sound the E and F#. Use your ear and the online audio to help check your **intonation** (accuracy of pitch). The first three notes are a whole step apart, like "do-re-mi."

Second Finger on D String

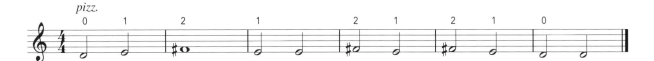

As you play "Putting It All Together," pluck the notes slowly, concentrating on finger placement and intonation. Gradually play faster as you get more comfortable. When the notes become easy, use the bowings given, but again, start slowly at first. Notice that in the fourth measure, we go from D up to F#, skipping E. When playing the F#, both fingers 1 and 2 will go down at the same time.

Putting It All Together

Once you are comfortable playing both *pizz.* and *arco* on this song, go back in the book and try playing the earlier songs *arco*.

Hot Cross Buns

► Now, you must play *pizz.* while holding the bow so it is ready for *arco* when you repeat. Curve your hand around the frog, still using the index finger to pluck.

The two dots next to the double bar line at the end are a repeat sign, meaning to go back to the beginning.

Rests

Rests indicate beats of silence.

Quarter Rest = 1 beat of silence—the same duration as a quarter note.

Half Rest = 2 beats of silence—the same duration as a half note.

Whole Rest = 4 beats of silence—the same duration as a whole note, or simply resting for a whole measure.

quarter rest	half rest	whole rest
(one beat)	(two beats)	(four beats)
		or whole measure

In "Mary's Lamb," use the rests in measures 2, 3, and 4 to lift and move the bow to again play down bow on beat one of the next measure.

Mary's Lamb

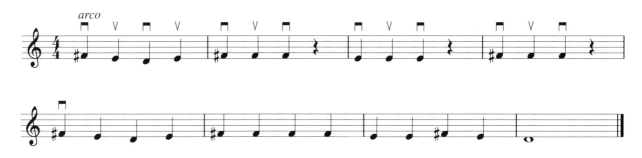

Notes on the A String

As we move over to the A string to learn some new notes, use "Open String Review" to refresh your memory on the note names. You may also use this as an opportunity to practice slightly lowering and raising your bow arm as you move from string to string to play each one clearly.

Open String Review

1st time pizz.
2nd time arco

New Note: B

First Finger on the A String: B – The note B sounds a whole step higher than open A string. Place your finger about 1 ¼ inches below the nut to sound the note B on the A string, in about the same place as you placed first finger on the D string in the last lesson.

B

Whole Step Happiness

pizz.

Whole Step Hoedown

pizz.

New Note: C♯

Second Finger on the A String: C♯ – The note C♯ sounds a whole step higher than first finger B. Place your second finger on the A string about one inch from the first finger, letting fingers 3 and 4 curve gently over the fingerboard. Remember to keep first finger down on the string while playing finger two.

C♯

Putting It All Together on the A String

► Listen to the whole steps between A and B, and B and C#. Use the audio to check your intonation.

Remember playing "Hot Cross Buns" on the D string? Now try playing it on the A string. Remember to always tighten the bow hair and rosin your bow before playing. Take a minute to check for a relaxed bow hold.

Hot Cross Buns in A

Key Signature – D

A key signature indicates what notes to play sharp or flat throughout an entire piece. When sharps are indicated in a key signature, they are no longer placed next to each note on the staff. A key signature with two sharps indicates that all written Fs and Cs should be played as sharps. This is the **Key of D**.

Now try "French Folk Song" with your bow. Notice that each measure begins down bow. In measure 4, lift your bow during the half rest so you can begin measure 5 down bow.

French Folk Song

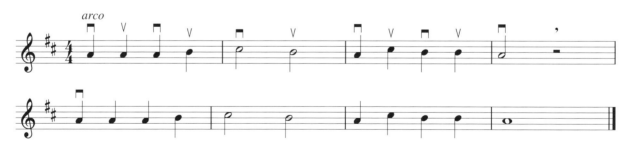

Lift and Breathe

The comma above the staff in "French Folk Song" is the sign to lift your bow. This is the same symbol used to tell wind instrument players to take a breath. This lift motion is also referred to as a *circle bow*, as you are making a circle in the air, returning the bow to the starting point for another down bow. As a string player, it is good to use these markings not only to lift the bow, but to breathe as well. Doing so helps promote a kind of natural phrasing to the song you are playing.

New Note on the D String: G

New Note: G

The note G sounds a half step higher than F#. This is a smaller **interval** than the whole steps you have been playing. To find the G on the D string, place finger three on the fingerboard right next to finger two. Fingers two and three should be slightly touching. Be sure that the fourth finger is curled over the fingerboard and not curled under.

As you are playing the next song, getting used to the new note G, practice slowly, playing *pizzicato*. Try playing it on your own, without the audio. When you are comfortable with it, play track 31 and try playing along.

New Note G Etude

Intervals

An interval is the distance between two pitches. So far, we have discussed the intervals half step and whole step. Your violin is tuned by another interval, the fifth. From bottom to top, each string is a fifth apart: G (a b c) D (e f g) A (b c d) E. To find any interval, count, beginning with the first pitch as one, and stop at your desired pitch. This number is the interval. For example, A up to C is a third: A (1), B (2), C (3), = 3rd.

Practice "D String Etude" *pizzicato* first, without holding the bow. Next, play *pizz.* while holding the bow. After that, practice *arco*, and when you are ready, try going from *pizz.* to *arco* on the repeat, without stopping.

D String Etude

By adding open string A to the notes you've learned on the D string, you can play a five-note **scale**. Keep finger 3 down on the D string as you play open A. This way you are ready to play finger 3 again, right away.

 # Five Note Scale

Always listen to yourself as you play to make sure you are in tune. What is the interval between D and A in the last measure? The intervals in the first three measures are all steps, but which are half steps, and which are whole steps?

Scales

A *scale* is a series of ascending or descending notes, arranged sequentially (following the alphabet, in order). The type of scale is defined by the intervals between each scale degree, primarily determined by which are half steps (**H**) and which are whole steps (**W**). For example, the arrangement of **W W H W W W H** is a **major scale**. If one begins on C, this scale would be all natural notes (no sharps or flats). To begin on D and follow this pattern would give us F sharp and C sharp. This D major scale is the basis for many of the tunes in this book.

"Bile 'em Cabbage" is a popular American fiddle tune. Keep a steady quarter-note beat using smooth longer bows for the half notes. The song is based on the notes of the D major scale. The entire D major scale will be introduced on page 21.

 # Bile 'em Cabbage

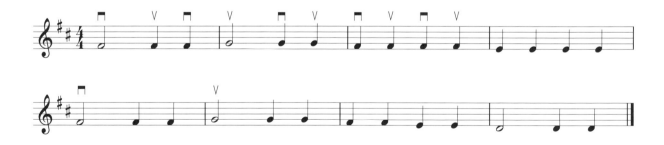

"Jingle Bells" uses notes on the D string and the open A string. When you are ready to try "Jingle Bells" with your bow, notice you will be lifting when there is a rest on beat 4, as in measures 4 and 12. Practice this motion in the air before putting your bow on the string.

Jingle Bells

In this theme from Dvořák's "New World Symphony," notice the line marked under the notes in measures 1–2, 3, and 5–6. This is a reminder that after playing finger 2 on F♯, you should keep finger 2 on the D string while you play the open A, coming right back to the F♯. Also note that during the rest in measure 4, you will lift your bow to begin down bow in measure 5.

New World Symphony Theme

Antonín Dvořák

New Note on the A String: D

New Note: D

The note D sounds a half step higher than C♯. To play a D on the A string, place your third finger on the A string right next to the second finger, with the second and third fingers slightly touching. This D is an **octave** higher than the open D string. Play open D and then D on the A string to compare the sound.

Play "High D–Low D" pizzicato, listening for the half step between C♯ and D, and the difference between the high and the low D.

High D–Low D

A String Etude

Notice the time signature in "Melody." There are 3 beats in each measure. Use a longer bow stroke to give the dotted half note 3 full beats.

Melody

Dynamics

Dynamics indicate how loud or soft the music will be played. Traditionally, dynamic terms are known by their Italian names:

p	*piano*	soft	*mp*	*mezzo piano*	moderately soft
f	*forte*	loud	*mf*	*mezzo forte*	moderately loud

Using a heavier bow stroke and a faster bow speed will create a louder tone. A slower bow speed and less weight on the bow will create a softer tone.

In "Aunt Rhody," note the change in dynamics. Start the piece with a strong bow stroke. In measure 7, use less weight for a softer sound.

 ## Aunt Rhody

 ## Playing the D Major Scale

You are now ready to play a D major scale. Starting with the open D string, play up to finger three, the note G. Continue, now starting on the open A string, going up to finger three, sounding the note D (an octave higher than where you started). Play the scale *pizzicato* with the audio to check for intonation. Play the scale *arco* when the fingering becomes easy. Next, try playing a descending scale—start with the high D and go down, playing the same notes you did on the way up.

 ## D Major Scale

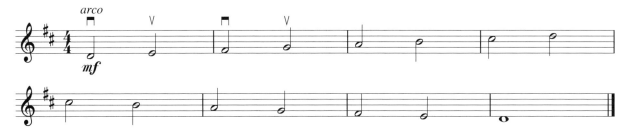

 ## Double Up

Notes on the E String

New Note: F#

The note F# sounds a whole step above open E string. Place your first finger on the E string about 1 ¼ inches below the nut to sound F#.

F#

Effortless F#

► With this new key signature, only the Fs are sharp.

Only one sharp in the key signature: G major

Whole Step Cha-Cha

Adding F# to the notes you are familiar with on the A string will enable you to play the following well-known folk tune.

Twinkle

► With this new key signature, all Fs, Cs, and Gs are played as sharps.

Three sharps: key of A major

New Note: G♯

Second Finger on the E String: G♯ – This note sounds a whole step above first finger F♯. Place your second finger on the E string about one inch from the first finger. Remember to keep fingers 3 and 4 curved over the fingerboard.

Whole Step Waltz

"Hungarian Folk Song" uses notes on both the E and A strings. Play slowly at first, and when you are comfortable with the notes and rhythms, try a lively tempo.

Hungarian Folk Song

Bartok

► Only the beginning down bow is given. Often a piece written mostly in quarter notes will use an alternating "down bow, up bow" pattern.

Long, Long Ago

► Be sure that your fingering hand remains in a relaxed, curved position as you move between the A and E strings.

Notes on the G String

New Note: A

The note A sounds a whole step higher than the open G string. Place your first finger on the G string about 1 ¼ inches below the nut to sound A. This A is one octave below the open string A. Remember to keep your fingers curved over the fingerboard.

A

New Note

New Note: B

The note B sounds a whole step higher than A. Place your second finger on the G string, about one inch from the first finger to sound B.

As you play "March on the G String," listen for whole steps between open G, A, and B. Check the time signature. How many beats are in each measure?

March on the G String

"G String Etude" uses notes on the G and D strings. Can you name all the notes?

 # G String Etude

Tempo Marking

Tempo refers to the speed at which a piece of music is played. In music, tempo markings are often indicated in Italian. A few common tempo indications include:

Allegro: fast

Moderato: moderate

Andante: slower "walking" tempo

Largo: very slow

Upbeat

Also called a "*pick-up note*," an *upbeat* is a note or notes that appear before the first full measure. The remaining beats are found at the end of the song. Should there be a repeat sign at the end, the last measure, combined with the first measure make up one complete measure when repeating back to the beginning without stopping.

 # Oh Susannah

The beautiful "Scottish Air," also known as "Annie Laurie," presents you with a new bowing challenge. Notice in measure two there are two up bows marked in a row. Use half of the bow for the half note, saving some bow to play the repeated E up bow on beat 4. This bowing pattern is also found in measures 6 and 14. Practice these measures separately to get a feel for this new bowing. Don't forget to begin the piece with an up bow on the first note.

Scottish Air

► Many different intervals are used in this song. Can you name them? Remember to check your tuning on all intervals.

The Octave

You've already learned the intervals half step, whole step, and fifth. Another important interval makes an appearance in "Scottish Air." The **octave** is the distance from one letter name, to the nearest note of the same letter name, i.e., G to the next G, up or down. In "Scottish Air," octaves appear in measures 1, 5, and 15. Two notes an octave apart have a certain "sameness" in sound. Watch carefully for octaves in all songs, and make sure you play them in tune.

Playing in Close Position

Up until now you have played fingers one, two, and three in just about the same place on each string. As you worked on learning the notes in these positions, you have realized that *where* you put your finger on the string affects the pitch. In this lesson, the placement of finger two on the D and A strings will change, creating new notes.

New Note: F

Close Position on the D String (low two): F (or "F natural," as opposed to F sharp).

To play F♮, which is only a half step higher than first finger E, place finger one to play an E and then place your second finger right next to the first finger. Fingers one and two should be slightly touching. This note is F♮. Some string players call this "low finger two," or two in "close" position, to distinguish it from finger two on the D string to play F♯ as you have previously learned. (F♮ is a half step lower than F sharp).

F

Natural Sign

A natural sign (♮) cancels a sharp or flat.

Low 2 Blues

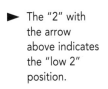

► The "2" with the arrow above indicates the "low 2" position.

Minor vs. Major

So far, we have learned about and played tunes in a major key. In general, major keys sound happy and bright. Minor keys sound sad and dark. Whether a tune is in major or minor depends largely on where the half steps are positioned in the scale—more about this in Level 2.

Try "Low Aunt Rhody" by playing all the F♯s as F♮s, with finger two in close position. Try playing it again with finger two playing F♯. Can you hear the difference? Playing the F♯ puts "Aunt Rhody" in a major key, while playing F♮ changes "Aunt Rhody" to a minor key.

"Low" Aunt Rhody

► Does this sound like Aunt Rhody is sad? If so, you're doing well with the "low 2."

New Note: C

To play C (or C natural), place finger two in close position on the A string. Remember that fingers one and two should be slightly touching.

C

 ## Close Friends

► Listen again to the sound of the half step between finger one and "low" finger two.

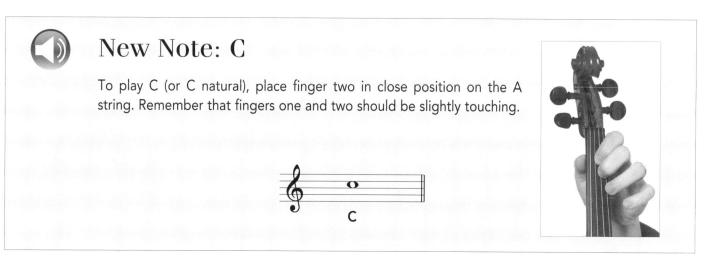

 ## German Folk Song

Can you find the C naturals in "Perfect Match"? Use a long bow stroke for the dotted half notes.

Perfect Match

"Folk Song" uses low finger two on both the D and A strings. Notice the absence of sharps in the key signature. There are arrows indicating low finger two above the F naturals and C naturals to help you focus on finger placement.

Folk Song

Are you ready for a challenge? "Bingo" uses C natural (low finger two on the A string) and F♯ (two on the D string).

Bingo

► Notice the repeat sign at the end. Make sure to return to the beginning without stopping.

Lesson 10 | Eighth Notes, Slurs, & Ties

An **eighth note** sounds for one half the value of a quarter note. Eighth notes often appear in music in groups of two or four beamed together. Two eighth notes equal the value of one quarter note.

♫ = ♩

Counting and Tapping

You may wish to tap your foot to help keep time and play eighth notes evenly. If your foot taps on each quarter-note beat, then consider the act of your foot lifting up as "in between the beat." Quarter notes would be played once on each tap. Eighth notes would be played one on each tap, and one on each lift of the foot, in between the taps.

Play the D scale below using eighth-note rhythms. Set a quarter-note beat to determine the speed of your eighth notes. Use about half of the bow for each quarter note, and smaller bow strokes for each eighth note.

Eighth Notes

Eighth notes can also be beamed in groups of 4 to make reading them easier.

Lightly Row

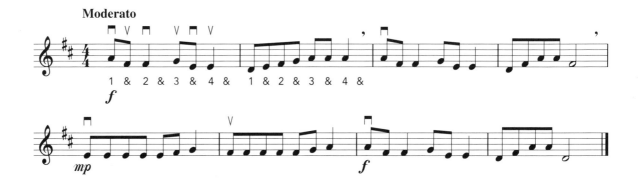

Look for the eighth notes in measures 10–11 of "Ode to Joy." Set a steady quarter-note beat using full bow strokes for the half notes, half bows for the quarter notes, and even shorter bows for the eighth notes.

Ode to Joy

Moderato

Beethoven

Slurs and Legato

String players often slur notes together, playing two or more notes with a single bow stroke. A **slur**, is a curved line connecting multiple notes, indicating this type of bowing.

Playing multiple notes in one bow stoke will cause the notes to sound smooth and connected. This style is known as **legato**.

Plenty to Slur

Andante

▶ Listen for a smooth connected sound between the two slurred notes.

Observe the Music

A helpful tip to aid in learning any piece of music is to spend some time looking at the music before ever playing a note. Look for anything tricky that may come up such as large interval skips, changing dynamics, or even a change in key or meter. It is also useful to look for repeated patterns within the music. Some measures may look like something that occurred earlier, but in fact might be slightly different. Being aware of these similarities and differences will help you prepare to play the tune.

"Country Gardens" contains many repeated patterns. Identifying these will help you to learn the piece more quickly.

 # Country Gardens

Practice Tips

"Caribbean Folk Song" is lively and fun to play. Some practice steps you may find useful include:

- Look at the music before playing, noticing every mark and symbol.
- Tap or clap the rhythm.
- Play *pizzicato* first to become familiar with the notes.
- Look ahead for slurs before bowing.

D.C. al Fine

D.C. stands for **Da Capo** which means "to the beginning." Fine means "end." When you see this sign, go back to the beginning of the song and play until Fine.

 # Caribbean Folk Song

The Tie

As you look through "Amazing Grace" you will notice two types of curved lines above and below the notes. We already know the slur, but another type of curved line often used in music is called a tie. This looks like a slur, but connects two notes that are the same pitch. A tie between two notes makes the first note last the value of both notes tied together. Thus, a dotted half note (3 beats) tied to a half note (2 beats) will be held for 5 beats. Many ties are used to extend notes beyond the bar line. Move the bow more slowly to hold the note for a full 5 beats.

Amazing Grace

► Be careful not to run out of bow when playing the long, tied notes.

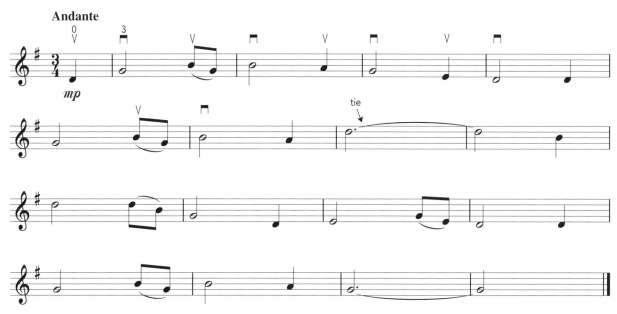

"Theme from Brahms Symphony No. 1" contains several challenges. First, note the key signature: F will be played as F♯ throughout this piece. C will be C natural—low finger two on the A string. Notice that each pair of eighth notes is slurred. You might try bowing those measures in the air to get a feel for the bow pattern before playing. Also, carefully practice the two up bows in a row in measure 8. This theme is played in an easy, stately manner.

Theme from Brahms Symphony No. 1

Brahms

Crescendo and Decrescendo (or "Diminuendo")

These are two musical terms that indicate a gradual change in dynamics or "dynamic shading." Crescendo means to gradually get louder. Decrescendo means to gradually get softer. Symbols represent these terms to make it easy to see exactly where, and for how long the change in dynamics should occur.

crescendo (cresc.) ⟨

decrescendo (decresc. or dim.) ⟩

Practice crescendo and decrescendo as you play the following open-string exercises. Take some time with these exercises as you learn to adjust and create the sound you desire.

 ## Open String Crescendo

 ## Open String Decrescendo

A long-note crescendo will often be played with an up bow. Decrescendos are more easily executed with a down bow. Though this bowing is common, the reverse is still possible, and sometimes unavoidable.

Open String Shading

Look ahead to see the crescendos and decrescendos in "Barbara Allen." Practice these measures separately until you achieve the sound you want. Also notice the single eighth note in the last measure. Count and tap this carefully.

Barbara Allen

Scottish Folk Song

In "Scarborough Fair," words are used to indicate crescendo and diminuendo instead of symbols. Decide where the loudest point of the crescendo will be in measures 8–10. Practice these measures until your crescendo and decrescendo are smooth and easy.

Scarborough Fair

English Folk Song

Two Duets

Finally, we will end with two duets. As you've played along with the audio so far, you were actually playing duets in that the audio tracks served as the second musician. With "When the Saints Go Marching In" and "Boatman Dance," this is your chance to find someone you know who also plays violin, and practice playing with another live musician. You will play the violin 1 part, and your friend, violin 2. Pay close attention to listening to each other. Both duets are also on the audio, so at first, you may both play along. When comfortable, try playing it together without the audio. Please note that the C♯ on the G string is included in the violin 2 part, a note not introduced in this book.

When the Saints Go Marching In (Duet)

Both Violin Parts

Violin 2, only

Traditional

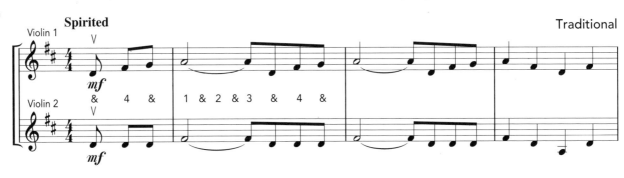

► On the second time through, ignore the tie in the last measure for a punctuated ending.

Boatman Dance (Duet)

American Folk Song

Fingering Chart

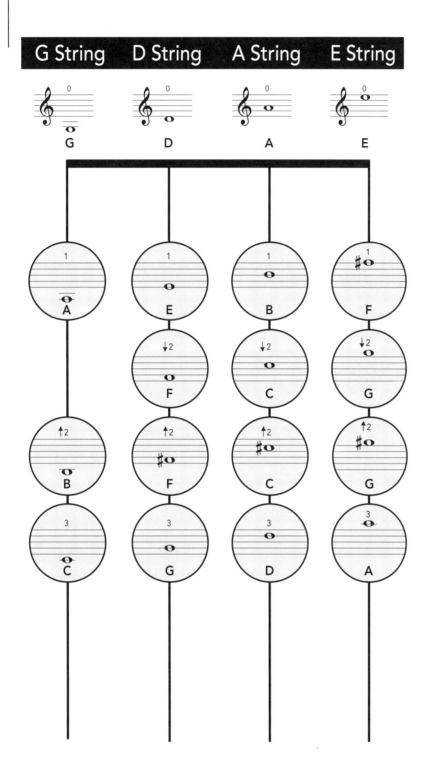

Glossary of Musical Terms

Accent	An Accent mark (>) means to emphasize the note to which it is attached.
Accidental	Any sharp (♯), flat (♭), or natural (♮) sign that appears in the music but is not in the key signature.
Allegro	Fast tempo.
Andante	Slower "walking" tempo.
Arco	With the bow.
Bass Clef (𝄢)	(F Clef) indicates the position of note names on a music staff. The fourth line in bass clef is F.
Bar Lines	Bar Lines divide the music staff into measures.
Beat	The pulse of music, like a heartbeat, should remain very steady. Counting aloud and foot-tapping help maintain a steady beat.
Breath Mark	The Breath Mark (') indicates a specific place to inhale or, on a string instrument, a place to lift the bow.
Chord	When two or more notes are played together, they form a chord or harmony.
Chromatic Notes	Chromatic Notes are altered with sharps, flats and natural signs which are not in the key signature.
Chromatic Scale	The smallest distance between two notes is a half step, and a scale made up of consecutive half steps is called a Chromatic Scale.
Common Time	Common Time (𝄴) is the same as ⁴⁄₄ time signature.
Crescendo	Play gradually louder. (*cresc.*)
D.C. al Fine	Play again from the beginning, stopping at Fine. D.C. is the abbreviation for Da Capo, or "to the beginning," and Fine means "the end."
Decrescendo	Play gradually softer. (*decresc.*)
Diminuendo	Same as decrescendo. (*dim.*)
Dotted Half Note	A note three beats long in duration. (♩.) A dot adds half the value of the original note.
Double Bar (𝄁)	Indicates the end of a piece of music.
Down Bow (⊓)	Drawing the bow downward, towards the floor.
Duet	A composition with two different parts played together.
Dynamics	Dynamics indicate how loud or soft to play a passage of music.
Eighth Note	An Eighth Note (♪) receives half the value of a quarter note, that is, half a beat. Two or more eighth notes are usually joined together with a beam, as follows: ♫
Eighth Rest	Indicates ½ beat of silence. (𝄾)
Enharmonics	Two notes that are written differently, but sound the same (and played with the same fingering) are called Enharmonics (F♯ and G♭).

Fermata	The Fermata (𝄐) indicates that a note (or rest) is held somewhat longer than normal.
Flat (♭)	Lowers the note a half step and remains in effect for the entire measure.
Forte (𝆑)	Play loudly.
Half Note	A Half Note (𝅗𝅥) receives two beats. It's equal in length to two quarter notes.
Half Rest	The Half Rest (𝄼) marks two beats of silence.
Harmony	Two or more notes played together.
Interval	The distance between two pitches.
Key Signature	A Key Signature (the group of sharps or flats before the time signature) tells which notes are played as sharps or flats throughout the entire piece.
Largo	A very slow tempo.
Ledger Lines	Ledger Lines extend the music staff. Notes on ledger lines can be above or below the staff.
Mezzo Forte (𝆐𝆑)	Moderately loud.
Mezzo Piano (𝆐𝆏)	Moderately soft.
Moderato	Medium or moderate tempo.
Music Staff	The Music Staff has 5 lines and 4 spaces where notes and rests are written.
Natural Sign (♮)	Cancels a flat ♭ or sharp ♯ and remains in effect for the entire measure.
Notes	Notes tell us how high or low to play by their placement on a line or space of the music staff, and how long to play.
Phrase	A Phrase is a musical "sentence," often 2 or 4 measures long.
Piano (𝆏)	Soft.
Pitch	The highness or lowness of a note which is indicated by the horizontal placement of the note on the music staff.
Pick-Up Notes	One or more notes that come before the first full measure. The beats of Pick-Up Notes are subtracted from the last measure—also called "upbeats."
Pizzicato	Plucked.
Quarter Note	A Quarter Note (♩) receives one beat. There are 4 quarter notes in a $\frac{4}{4}$ measure.
Quarter Rest	The Quarter Rest (𝄽) marks one beat of silence.
Repeat Sign	The Repeat Sign (𝄇) means to play once again from the beginning without pause. Repeat the section of music enclosed by the repeat signs (𝄆 𝄇). If 1st and 2nd endings are used, they are played as usual—but go back only to the first repeat sign, not to the beginning.

Rests	Beats of silence.
Rhythm	Rhythm refers to time—how long, or for how many beats a note lasts, including rests.
Scale	A sequence of notes in ascending or descending order. Like a musical "ladder," each step is the next consecutive note in the musical alphabet.
Sharp (♯)	Raises the note a half step and remains in effect for the entire measure.
Slur	A curved line connecting notes of different pitch.
Tempo	The speed of music.
Tie	A curved line connecting two notes of the same pitch. A tie between two notes makes the first note last the value of both notes "tied" together.
Time Signature	Indicates how many beats per measure and what kind of note gets one beat.
Treble Clef (𝄞)	(G Clef) indicates the position of note names on a music staff: The second line in Treble Clef is G.
Up Bow (∨)	Drawing the bow upward, towards you
Upbeat	See "pick-up note."
Whole Note	A Whole Note (𝅝) lasts for four full beats (a complete measure in $\frac{4}{4}$ time).
Whole Rest	The Whole Rest (▬) indicates a whole measure of silence.